HAVING
FUN
WITH
BIBLE
PUZZLES

THOMAS N. HORTON

BROADMAN PRESS
NASHVILLE, TENNESSEE

To my parents,
Bill and Maynell

© Copyright 1990 ● Broadman Press
All rights reserved
4291-16

ISBN: 0-8054-9116-3
Dewey Decimal Classification: 220
Subject Heading: BIBLE - QUESTION BOOKS

Printed in the United States of America

The *New American Standard Bible*, ©The Lockman Foundation, 1960, 1962, 1963, 1968, 1971, 1973, 1975, 1977 was used to prepare these puzzles.

Contents

Acrostic

The first letter of each acrostic puzzle is given for you.
The correct number of blanks is shown for each missing word.

1
Old Testament Books

Complete the acrostic by naming the Old Testament book for each line.

Hint: one book is found in the New Testament.

```
A __ __ __
P __ __ __ __ __
O __ __ __ __ __ __
S __ __ __        __ __        __ __ __ __ __ __ __
T __ __ __ __
L __ __ __ __ __ __ __ __ __ __
E __ __ __
```

2
The Great Plagues

Complete the acrostic by naming the words associated with the great plagues in Egypt.

Exodus 7:17	W __ __ __ __
Exodus 11:5	O __ __ __ __ __
Exodus 10:19	R __ __ __ __ __
Exodus 7:10	S __ __ __ __ __ __
Exodus 9:18	H __ __ __
Exodus 8:21	I __ __ __ __ __ __
Exodus 9:8	P __ __ __ __ __ __

3
Places of the Bible

Complete the acrostic by naming the place, city, or country for each line.

Acts 28:14   R __ __ __
Genesis 2:8   E __ __ __
Revelation 1:9   P __ __ __ __ __
Genesis 39:1   E __ __ __ __
Jonah 1:2   N __ __ __ __ __ __
Joshua 19:29   T __ __ __

4
Sins

Complete the acrostic by naming some of the sins that we should avoid in our Christian lives.

Romans 1:29	D __ __ __ __ __
1 Peter 2:1	E __ __ __
Psalms 119:37	V __ __ __ __ __
1 Corinthians 10:14	I __ __ __ __ __ __ __
John 8:44	L __ __

5
Food of the Bible

Complete the acrostic by naming the various foods mentioned in the Bible.

2 Samuel 16:1	B __ __ __ __
Deuteronomy 22:6	E __ __ __
Genesis 43:11	A __ __ __ __ __ __
Genesis 43:11	N __ __ __
Job 6:6	S __ __ __

6
The First Garden

Complete the acrostic by naming the words associated with the first garden.

Genesis 1:1	G __ __
Genesis 2:8	E __ __ __
Genesis 4:16	N __ __
Genesis 2:17	E __ __ __
Genesis 3:1	S __ __ __ __ __ __
Genesis 1:26	I __ __ __ __
Genesis 4:7	S __ __

7
New Testament Books

Complete the acrostic by naming the New Testament book for each line.

G _ _ _ _ _ _ _ _
R _ _ _ _ _ _ _ _ _
A _ _ _
C _ _ _ _ _ _ _ _ _
E _ _ _ _ _ _ _ _

8
Names for Christ

Complete the acrostic by naming the various names for Christ.

Hebrews 1:6	F _ _ _ _
1 John 2:1	A _ _ _ _ _ _ _
Matthew 1:23	I _ _ _ _ _ _ _
Mark 12:14	T _ _ _ _ _ _
Colossians 1:27	H _ _ _

9
Passover Dinner

Complete the acrostic by naming the words associated with the last Passover.

John 13:2	S	__ __ __ __ __
Luke 22:1	U	__ __ __ __ __ __ __ __ __
Luke 22:1	P	__ __ __ __ __ __ __
Luke 22:10	P	__ __ __ __ __ __
Matthew 26:26	E	__ __
Matthew 26:20	R	__ __ __ __ __ __ __ __

10
Christ's Death

Complete the acrostic by naming the words associated with the crucifixion.

John 19:2	C __ __ __ __
John 11:25	R __ __ __ __ __ __ __ __ __ __ __
Matthew 27:52	O __ __ __ __ __
John 20:1	S __ __ __ __
Luke 23:33	S __ __ __ __

Word Jumble

Unscramble each jumbled word to form ordinary words.
Place one letter in each blank.
Then write each letter that is underscored twice in the blanks at
the bottom of the puzzle. Unscramble the bonus word.

11
Who Was David's Best Friend?

Hint: the words have something to do with David's life.

1. M O O O N L S

___ ___ ___ ___ ___ ___ ⹀

2. E S S J E

⹀ ___ ___ ___ ___

3. E T P E M L

⹀ ___ ___ ___ ___ ___

4. L H G I A O T

___ ⹀ ___ ___ ___ ___ ⹀

5. N I G K

___ ___ ⹀ ___

6. T B H E A B A H S

___ ⹀ ___ ___ ___ ___ ___ ___ ⹀

Scrambled word   ___ ___ ___ ___ ___ ___ ___

Bonus word   ___ ___ ___ ___ ___ ___ ___

12
Which Prophet Was Fed By Ravens?

The following scrambled words are names of prophets found in the Old Testament.

1. E L O J

   _ _ _ _
   _

2. N H E O C

   _ _ _ _ _
       _

3. J L H I A E

   _ _ _ _ _ _
         _

4. H N N A A T

   _ _ _ _ _ _
           _

5. M C H I A

   _ _ _ _ _
         _

6. H U A M N

   _ _ _ _ _

Scrambled word   _ _ _ _ _

Bonus word   _ _ _ _ _

13
Where Was Egypt's Army Destroyed?

The following scrambled words are names of rivers found in the Old Testament.

1. I T S I G R

   __ __ __ __ __ __
       __

2. L I E N

   __ __ __ __
       __

3. D N O R A J

   __ __ __ __ __ __
       __

4. E A T S P E H U R

   __ __ __ __ __ __ __ __ __
       __

5. N N A O R

   __ __ __ __ __
       __

6. S I N P O H

   __ __ __ __ __ __
       __

Scrambled word   __ __ __   __ __ __

Bonus word   __ __ __   __ __ __

14
Where Did the Sun Stand Still?

The following scrambled words are names of soldiers found in the Old Testament.

1. R A H I U

   _ _ _ _ _

2. A B J O

   _ _ _ _

   _

3. A J U O S H

   _ _ _ _ _ _

   _

4. A D D V I

   _ _ _ _ _

   _

5. B R E A N

   _ _ _ _ _

   _ _

6. E E L G N R A

   _ _ _ _ _ _ _

   _

Scrambled word   _ _ _ _ _ _

Bonus word   _ _ _ _ _ _

15
Which Angel Spoke to Mary About Jesus' Birth?

The following scrambled words are names of women found in the Old Testament.

1. S E E R H T

   __ __ __ __ __
   __

2. A A I I L G B

   __ __ __ __ __ __ __
   __

3. E A L L H D I

   __ __ __ __ __ __ __
   __ __

4. L R H A C E

   __ __ __ __ __ __
   __

5. G H R A A

   __ __ __ __ __
   __

6. M G E O R

   __ __ __ __ __
   __

Scrambled word   __ __ __ __ __ __ __

Bonus word   __ __ __ __ __ __ __

16
What Represented "Sons of the Evil One" in the Parable?

The following scrambled words are words that are found in the parables of Jesus.

1. N E L V E A

  — — — — — —
      —

2. O I D W W

  — — — — —

3. O E R S W

  — — — — —
      —

4. E U H S O

  — — — — —
      —

5. A I S M A A R T N

  — — — — — — — —
  —

6. S T T N E A L

  — — — — — —
      —

Scrambled word   — — — — —

Bonus word   — — — — —

17
Who Was Peter's Brother?

The following scrambled words are words that we associate with Peter's life.

1. O S M N I

_ _ _ _ _
        _

2. E W T R A

_ _ _ _ _
_   _

3. T C E S O E P T N

_ _ _ _ _ _ _ _ _
    _

4. R C O A S D

_ _ _ _ _ _
_

5. A E O T P S L

_ _ _ _ _ _ _
_

6. K O C C

_ _ _ _

Scrambled word   _ _ _ _ _ _

Bonus word   _ _ _ _ _ _

18
The Christian Life

The following scrambled words identify what we should experience in our Christian lives.

1. T E N C I P E A

—— —— —— —— =—— —— ——

2. O S I W M D

—— —— —— == == ——

3. R R Y P E A

—— —— —— —— —— ——

4. T F I A H

—— —— == —— ——

5. C R Y E M

—— —— —— —— ——

6. E N A R E C T E P N

—— —— —— == —— —— —— —— ——

7. N I S E C O S N O F

== —— —— == —— —— —— —— —— ——

8. R S A L I T

—— —— —— —— —— ——

9. U G I R O S T S E N S E H

—— —— —— —— —— —— == —— —— —— —— —— ——

10. T M I P A S B

== —— —— —— —— —— ——

Scrambled word —— —— —— —— —— —— —— —— ——

Bonus word —— —— —— —— —— —— —— —— ——

22

19
Who Carried Jesus' Cross?

The following scrambled words are words having to do with the crucifixion.

1. E P T A L I

   _ _ _ _ _ _
       _

2. O D B O L

   _ _ _ _ _
       _

3. S S R C O

   _ _ _ _ _
         _

4. O T G A H L O G

   _ _ _ _ _ _ _ _

5. A E T G N S R M

   _ _ _ _ _ _ _ _
             _

6. N R C W O

   _ _ _ _ _
           _

Scrambled word   _ _ _ _ _

Bonus word   _ _ _ _ _

20
On Which Road Was Paul Converted?

The following scrambled words are terms concerning Paul's life.

1. U A L S

_ _ _ _
_ _

2. S I A A N N A

_ _ _ _ _ _ _
_

3. N A C O O L S S S I

_ _ _ _ _ _ _ _ _ _
_ _

4. K E A T R E N T M

_ _ _ _ _ _ _ _ _
_

5. I L S S A

_ _ _ _ _
_

6. D D N E L B I

_ _ _ _ _ _ _
_

Scrambled word   _ _ _ _ _ _ _ _

Bonus word   _ _ _ _ _ _ _ _

Matching

Match column A with column B.
Use the specific instructions before each puzzle to help.

21
Extra! Extra! Read All About It in the Old Testament

Match the book of the Bible where someone can read all about
each headline.

A	B
1. Moses receives the Ten Commandments.	a. Judges
2. David becomes King.	b. 2 Kings
3. Samson slays 1,000 Philistines with a jawbone.	c. Joshua
4. Aaron dies.	d. Genesis
5. The sun stands still.	e. 2 Samuel
6. Shadrach, Meshach, and Abed-nego survive the furnace.	f. Jonah
7. A flood destroys the earth.	g. Exodus
8. Solomon builds a temple.	h. Daniel
9. Elijah is carried away by a whirlwind.	i. 1 Kings
10. Man swallowed by a great fish.	j. Numbers

22
Bible Numbers

Match the description in column A with the correct quantity in column B.

A	B
1. Books in the Old Testament	a. 430
2. Tribes of Israel	b. 11
3. One-chapter books in the Old Testament	c. 3
4. Psalms	d. 52
5. Noah's sons	e. 12
6. Chapters in the Book of Isaiah	f. 39
7. Joseph's brothers	g. 7
8. Years the sons of Israel lived in Egypt	h. 150
9. Years Solomon took to build the temple	i. 1
10. Days Nehemiah took to build the wall	j. 66

23
Brothers

Match the name in column A with his brother in column B.

A	B
1. Jacob	a. Ephraim
2. Manasseh	b. Shem
3. Reuben	c. Aaron
4. Moses	d. Benjamin
5. Japheth	e. David
6. Eliab	f. Esau

24

Fathers and Sons

Match the father in column A with his son in column B.

A	B
1. David	a. Gershom
2. Moses	b. Abraham
3. Israel	c. Absalom
4. Cain	d. Reuben
5. Lamech	e. Enoch
6. Terah	f. Noah

25
Husbands and Wives

Match the husband in column A with his wife in column B.

A	B
1. Uriah	a. Abigail
2. Aquila	b. Priscilla
3. Jacob	c. Mary
4. Joseph—Old Test.	d. Bathsheba
5. David	e. Leah
6. Joseph—New Test.	f. Asenath

26
Rulers

Match the Ruler in column A with one of his acts in column B.

A	B
1. Solomon	a. Had 88 children.
2. David	b. Allowed Nehemiah to leave to build the wall.
3. Hezekiah	c. Took Esther as his queen.
4. Nebuchadnezzar	d. Took a census and made God angry.
5. Artaxerxes	e. Had a son named Jonathan.
6. Ahasuerus	f. Ate grass like cattle.
7. Rehoboam	g. God added 15 years to his life.
8. Saul	h. Had an alliance with King Hiram to build the temple.

27
People and Places

Match the person in column A with the place associated with him in column B.

A	B
1. Mary	a. Island of Patmos
2. John the Baptist	b. Cyprus
3. John the Apostle	c. Golgotha
4. Peter	d. Ephesus
5. Judas	e. Bethlehem
6. Barnabas	f. Sea of Galilee
7. Aquila	g. Gethsemane
8. Jesus	h. Jordan River

Decode

Decode each Bible verse using the code below.
Write the letter or word in each blank that matches its number or letter code.

Use the following code.

1 - A	9 - I	16 - Q
2 - B	10 - K	17 - R
3 - C	11 - L	18 - S
4 - D	12 - M	19 - T
5 - E	13 - N	20 - U
6 - F	14 - O	21 - V
7 - G	15 - P	22 - W
8 - H		23 - Y

A - and	C - Lord	E - the
B - but	D - to	F - for

Prayer
28

___ ___ ___ , ___ (A) ___ ___ ___ ___ ___ ___ ___ ___
1 18 10   (A)   9 19   18 8 1 11 11

___ ___ ___ ___ ___ ___ ___ ___ (D) ___ ___ ___ ___ ;
2 5   7 9 21 5 13   (D)   23 14 20

___ ___ ___ ___ , ___ (A) ___ ___ ___
18 5 5 10   (A)   23 14 20

___ ___ ___ ___ ___ ___ ___ ___ ___ ;
18 8 1 11 11   6 9 13 4

___ ___ ___ ___ ___ , ___ (A) ___ ___
10 13 14 3 10   (A)   9 19

___ ___ ___ ___ ___ ___ ___ ___ ___ ___ ___ ___
18 8 1 11 11   2 5   14 15 5 13 5 4

___ ___ ___ ___ ___ ___ .
(D)   23 14 20

32

29
Gentle Answers

$\overline{1}$ $\overline{7}$ $\overline{5}$ $\overline{13}$ $\overline{19}$ $\overline{11}$ $\overline{5}$ $\overline{1}$ $\overline{13}$ $\overline{18}$ $\overline{22}$ $\overline{5}$ $\overline{17}$,

$\overline{19}$ $\overline{20}$ $\overline{17}$ $\overline{13}$ $\overline{18}$ $\overline{1}$ $\overline{22}$ $\overline{1}$ $\overline{23}$ $\overline{22}$ $\overline{17}$ $\overline{1}$ $\overline{19}$ $\overline{8}$,

$\overline{(}$ $\overline{B}$ $\overline{)}$ $\overline{1}$ $\overline{8}$ $\overline{1}$ $\overline{17}$ $\overline{18}$ $\overline{8}$ $\overline{22}$ $\overline{14}$ $\overline{17}$ $\overline{4}$

$\overline{18}$ $\overline{19}$ $\overline{9}$ $\overline{17}$ $\overline{18}$ $\overline{20}$ $\overline{15}$ $\overline{1}$ $\overline{13}$ $\overline{7}$ $\overline{5}$ $\overline{17}$.

30
Strength

$\overline{9}$ $\quad\overline{3}$ $\quad\overline{1}$ $\quad\overline{13}$ $\quad\overline{4}$ $\quad\overline{14}$ $\qquad\overline{1}$ $\quad\overline{11}$ $\quad\overline{11}$

$\overline{19}$ $\quad\overline{8}$ $\quad\overline{9}$ $\quad\overline{13}$ $\quad\overline{7}$ $\quad\overline{18}$

$\overline{19}$ $\quad\overline{8}$ $\quad\overline{17}$ $\quad\overline{14}$ $\quad\overline{20}$ $\quad\overline{7}$ $\quad\overline{8}$ $\qquad\overline{8}$ $\quad\overline{9}$ $\quad\overline{12}$ $\qquad\overline{22}$ $\quad\overline{8}$ $\quad\overline{14}$

$\overline{18}$ $\quad\overline{19}$ $\quad\overline{17}$ $\quad\overline{5}$ $\quad\overline{13}$ $\quad\overline{7}$ $\quad\overline{19}$ $\quad\overline{8}$ $\quad\overline{5}$ $\quad\overline{13}$ $\quad\overline{18}$ $\qquad\overline{12}$ $\quad\overline{5}$.

31
Prophecy

__ __ __ __ __ __ __ __ __ __ __ __
(F) 13 14   15 17 14 15 8 5 3 23

__ __ __ __ __ __ __ __ __ __ __ __ __
22 1 18   5 21 5 17   12 1 4 5   2 23

__ __ __ __ __ __ __ __ __ __ __ __
1 13   1 3 19   14 6   8 20 12 1 13

__ __ __ __ __ __ __ __ __ __
22 9 11 11 ' (B)   12 5 13

__ __ __ __ __
12 14 21 5 4

__ __ __ __ __ __ __ __ __
2 23   (E)   8 14 11 23

__ __ __ __ __ __
18 15 9 17 9 19

__ __ __ __ __ __ __ __ __ __ __ __ .
18 15 14 10 5   6 17 14 12   7 14 4

32
God Is Giving

(F)   (E)   (C)   7 14 4

9 18   1   18 20 13   (A)

18 8 9 5 11 4 ;

(E)   (C)   7 9 21 5 18

7 17 1 3 5   (A)   7 11 14 17 23 ;

13 14

7 14 14 4   19 8 9 13 7   4 14 5 18

8 5

22 9 19 8 8 14 11 4   6 17 14 12

19 8 14 18 5

22 8 14   22 1 11 10   20 15 17 9 7

8 19 11 23 .

33
Eternal Life

$\overline{19}\ \overline{8}\ \overline{5}\ \overline{18}\ \overline{5}\quad \overline{19}\ \overline{8}\ \overline{9}\ \overline{13}\ \overline{7}\ \overline{18}\quad \overline{9}$

$\overline{8}\ \overline{1}\ \overline{21}\ \overline{5}\quad \overline{22}\ \overline{17}\ \overline{9}\ \overline{19}\ \overline{19}\ \overline{5}\ \overline{13}\quad (\ D\ )$

$\overline{23}\ \overline{14}\ \overline{20}\quad \overline{22}\ \overline{8}\ \overline{14}\quad \overline{2}\ \overline{5}\ \overline{11}\ \overline{9}\ \overline{5}\ \overline{21}\ \overline{5}$

$\overline{9}\ \overline{13}\quad (\ E\ )\quad \overline{13}\ \overline{1}\ \overline{12}\ \overline{5}\quad \overline{14}\ \overline{6}\quad (\ E\ )$

$\overline{18}\ \overline{14}\ \overline{13}\quad \overline{14}\ \overline{6}\quad \overline{7}\ \overline{14}\ \overline{4}\ ,\ \overline{9}\ \overline{13}$

$\overline{14}\ \overline{17}\ \overline{4}\ \overline{5}\ \overline{17}\quad \overline{19}\ \overline{8}\ \overline{1}\ \overline{19}\quad \overline{23}\ \overline{14}\ \overline{20}$

$\overline{12}\ \overline{1}\ \overline{23}$

$\overline{10}\ \overline{13}\ \overline{14}\ \overline{22}\quad \overline{19}\ \overline{8}\ \overline{1}\ \overline{19}\quad \overline{23}\ \overline{14}\ \overline{20}$

$\overline{8}\ \overline{1}\ \overline{21}\ \overline{5}$

$\overline{5}\ \overline{19}\ \overline{5}\ \overline{17}\ \overline{13}\ \overline{1}\ \overline{11}\quad \overline{11}\ \overline{9}\ \overline{6}\ \overline{5}\ .$

34
God Has Plans

__ __ __   __   __ __ __ __   __ __ __
(F)   9   10 13 14 22   (E)

__ __ __ __ __
15 11 1 13 18

__ __ __ __   __   __ __ __ __   __ __ __
19 8 1 19   9   8 1 21 5   (F)

__ __ __ ,
23 14 20

__ __ __ __ __ __ __ __   __ __ __   __ __ __ ,
4 5 3 11 1 17 5 18   (E)   (C)

__ __ __ __ __   __ __ __
15 11 1 13 18   (F)

__ __ __ __ __ __ __
22 5 11 6 1 17 5

__ __ __   __ __ __   __ __ __
(A)   13 14 19   (F)

__ __ __ __ __ __ __ __
3 1 11 1 12 9 19 23

__ __ __   __ __ __ __   __ __ __   __
(D)   7 9 21 5   23 14 20   1

__ __ __ __ __ __
6 20 19 20 17 5

__ __ __   __   __ __ __ __ .
(A)   1   8 14 15 5

38

35
Scripture

$\overline{1}$ $\overline{11}$ $\overline{11}$ $\quad$ $\overline{18}$ $\overline{3}$ $\overline{17}$ $\overline{9}$ $\overline{15}$ $\overline{19}$ $\overline{20}$ $\overline{17}$ $\overline{5}$ $\quad$ $\overline{9}$ $\overline{18}$

$\overline{9}$ $\overline{13}$ $\overline{18}$ $\overline{15}$ $\overline{9}$ $\overline{17}$ $\overline{5}$ $\overline{4}$ $\quad$ $\overline{2}$ $\overline{23}$ $\quad$ $\overline{7}$ $\overline{14}$ $\overline{4}$

$\overline{(}$ $\overline{A}$ $\overline{)}$ $\quad$ $\overline{15}$ $\overline{17}$ $\overline{14}$ $\overline{6}$ $\overline{9}$ $\overline{19}$ $\overline{1}$ $\overline{2}$ $\overline{11}$ $\overline{5}$

$\overline{(}$ $\overline{F}$ $\overline{)}$

$\overline{19}$ $\overline{5}$ $\overline{1}$ $\overline{3}$ $\overline{8}$ $\overline{9}$ $\overline{13}$ $\overline{7}$, $\overline{(}$ $\overline{F}$ $\overline{)}$

$\overline{17}$ $\overline{5}$ $\overline{15}$ $\overline{17}$ $\overline{14}$ $\overline{14}$ $\overline{6}$, $\overline{(}$ $\overline{F}$ $\overline{)}$

$\overline{3}$ $\overline{14}$ $\overline{17}$ $\overline{17}$ $\overline{5}$ $\overline{3}$ $\overline{19}$ $\overline{9}$ $\overline{14}$ $\overline{13}$, $\overline{(}$ $\overline{F}$ $\overline{)}$

$\overline{19}$ $\overline{17}$ $\overline{1}$ $\overline{9}$ $\overline{13}$ $\overline{9}$ $\overline{13}$ $\overline{7}$ $\quad$ $\overline{9}$ $\overline{13}$

$\overline{17}$ $\overline{9}$ $\overline{7}$ $\overline{8}$ $\overline{19}$ $\overline{5}$ $\overline{14}$ $\overline{20}$ $\overline{18}$ $\overline{13}$ $\overline{5}$ $\overline{18}$ $\overline{18}$.

36
Our Sin

$\overline{1}$ $\overline{11}$ $\overline{11}$ $\overline{14}$ $\overline{6}$ $\overline{20}$ $\overline{18}$ $\overline{11}$ $\overline{9}$ $\overline{10}$ $\overline{5}$

$\overline{18}$ $\overline{8}$ $\overline{5}$ $\overline{5}$ $\overline{15}$ $\overline{8}$ $\overline{1}$ $\overline{21}$ $\overline{5}$ $\overline{7}$ $\overline{14}$ $\overline{13}$ $\overline{5}$

$\overline{1}$ $\overline{18}$ $\overline{19}$ $\overline{17}$ $\overline{1}$ $\overline{23}$, $\overline{5}$ $\overline{1}$ $\overline{3}$ $\overline{8}$ $\overline{14}$ $\overline{6}$ $\overline{20}$ $\overline{18}$

$\overline{8}$ $\overline{1}$ $\overline{18}$ $\overline{19}$ $\overline{20}$ $\overline{17}$ $\overline{13}$ $\overline{5}$ $\overline{4}$ $\overline{(\ D\ )}$

$\overline{8}$ $\overline{9}$ $\overline{18}$

$\overline{14}$ $\overline{22}$ $\overline{13}$ $\overline{22}$ $\overline{1}$ $\overline{23}$; $\overline{(\ B\ )}$ $\overline{(\ E\ )}$

$\overline{(\ C\ )}$

$\overline{8}$ $\overline{1}$ $\overline{18}$ $\overline{3}$ $\overline{1}$ $\overline{20}$ $\overline{18}$ $\overline{5}$ $\overline{4}$ $\overline{(\ E\ )}$

$\overline{9}$ $\overline{13}$ $\overline{9}$ $\overline{16}$ $\overline{20}$ $\overline{9}$ $\overline{19}$ $\overline{23}$ $\overline{14}$ $\overline{6}$ $\overline{20}$ $\overline{18}$

$\overline{1}$ $\overline{11}$ $\overline{11}$

$\overline{(\ D\ )}$ $\overline{6}$ $\overline{1}$ $\overline{11}$ $\overline{11}$ $\overline{14}$ $\overline{13}$ $\overline{8}$ $\overline{9}$ $\overline{12}$.

37
Forgiveness

$\overline{9}$ $\overline{6}$ $\overline{22}$ $\overline{5}$ $\overline{3}$ $\overline{14}$ $\overline{13}$ $\overline{6}$ $\overline{5}$ $\overline{18}$ $\overline{18}$ $\overline{14}$ $\overline{20}$ $\overline{17}$

$\overline{18}$ $\overline{9}$ $\overline{13}$ $\overline{18}$, $\overline{8}$ $\overline{5}$ $\overline{9}$ $\overline{18}$

$\overline{6}$ $\overline{1}$ $\overline{9}$ $\overline{19}$ $\overline{8}$ $\overline{6}$ $\overline{20}$ $\overline{11}$

$\overline{(\;A\;)}$ $\overline{17}$ $\overline{9}$ $\overline{7}$ $\overline{8}$ $\overline{19}$ $\overline{5}$ $\overline{14}$ $\overline{20}$ $\overline{18}$

$\overline{(\;D\;)}$

$\overline{6}$ $\overline{14}$ $\overline{17}$ $\overline{7}$ $\overline{9}$ $\overline{21}$ $\overline{5}$ $\overline{20}$ $\overline{18}$ $\overline{14}$ $\overline{20}$ $\overline{17}$

$\overline{18}$ $\overline{9}$ $\overline{13}$ $\overline{18}$

$\overline{(\;A\;)}$ $\overline{(\;D\;)}$ $\overline{3}$ $\overline{11}$ $\overline{5}$ $\overline{1}$ $\overline{13}$ $\overline{18}$ $\overline{5}$

$\overline{20}$ $\overline{18}$

$\overline{6}$ $\overline{17}$ $\overline{14}$ $\overline{12}$ $\overline{1}$ $\overline{11}$ $\overline{11}$ $\overline{20}$ $\overline{13}$ $\overline{17}$ $\overline{9}$ $\overline{7}$ $\overline{8}$ $\overline{19}$

$\overline{5}$ $\overline{14}$ $\overline{20}$ $\overline{18}$ $\overline{13}$ $\overline{5}$ $\overline{18}$ $\overline{18}$.

Fill in the Blanks

The following puzzles are Bible verses in which some key words have been omitted.
Each blank is numbered with a corresponding number below the puzzle.
Write the correct word in the blanks below the puzzle.

38
Trust

(1) in the (2) with all your (3),
And do not (4) on your (5) (6).
In all your (7) (8) Him,
And He will make your (9) (10).

1. _____
2. _____
3. _____
4. _____
5. _____
6. _____
7. _____
8. _____
9. _____
10. _____

39
Praise God

(1) (2) to the Lord, all the (3).
(4) the Lord with (5);
(6) before Him with (7) (8).
(9) that the Lord (10) is God;
It is He who has (11) us, and not we (12);
We are (13) (14) and the (15) of His pasture.

1.	_____	9.	_____
2.	_____	10.	_____
3.	_____	11.	_____
4.	_____	12.	_____
5.	_____	13.	_____
6.	_____	14.	_____
7.	_____	15.	_____
8.	_____		

The Law

"You shall have no other (1) before (2).

"You shall not make for yourself an (3), or any (4) of what is in (5) above or on the earth beneath or in the (6) under the earth.

"You shall not (7) them or (8) them; for I, the Lord your God, am a (9) God, visiting the (10) of the fathers on the children, on the third and fourth (11) of those who (12) Me, but showing (13) to thousands, to those who (14) Me and (15) My commandments.

"You shall not take the (16) of the Lord your God in (17), for the Lord will not leave him (18) who takes His (19) in (20).

"Remember the (21) day, to keep it (22).

"(23) days you shall labor and do all your work, but the (24) day is a (25) of the Lord your God; in it you shall not do any work, you or your son or your daughter, your male or your female servant or your (26) or your sojourner who stays with you.

"For in (27) days the Lord made the (28) and the (29), the (30) and all that is in them, and rested on the (31) day; therefore the Lord blessed the (32) day and made it (33).

"(34) your father and your mother, that your days may be (35) in the land which the Lord your God gives you.

"You shall not (36).

"You shall not (37) (38).

" You shall not (39).

"You shall not bear (40) (41) against your neighbor.

"You shall not (42) your neighbor's house; you shall not covet your neighbor's (43) or his male servant or his female servant or his ox or his donkey or anything that (44) to your neighbor."

1. _____   23. _____
2. _____   24. _____
3. _____   25. _____
4. _____   26. _____
5. _____   27. _____
6. _____   28. _____
7. _____   29. _____
8. _____   30. _____
9. _____   31. _____
10. _____   32. _____
11. _____   33. _____
12. _____   34. _____
13. _____   35. _____
14. _____   36. _____
15. _____   37. _____
16. _____   38. _____
17. _____   39. _____
18. _____   40. _____
19. _____   41. _____
20. _____   42. _____
21. _____   43. _____
22. _____   44. _____

41
The Beatitudes

"Blessed are the (1) in spirit, for theirs is the (2) of heaven.

"Blessed are those who (3), for they shall be (4).

"Blessed are the (5), for they shall (6) the earth.

"Blessed are those who (7) and (8) for (9), for they shall be (10).

"Blessed are the (11), for they shall receive (12).

"Blessed are the (13) in heart, for they shall (14) God.

"Blessed are the (15), for they shall be called (16) of God.

"Blessed are those who have been (17) for the sake of (18), for theirs is the (19) of (20).

"Blessed are you when (21) (22) you, and (23) you, and say all kinds of (24) against you (25), on account of Me.

"(26), and be glad, for your (27) in heaven is great, for so they (28) the (29) who were before you."

1. _____	11. _____	21. _____
2. _____	12. _____	22. _____
3. _____	13. _____	23. _____
4. _____	14. _____	24. _____
5. _____	15. _____	25. _____
6. _____	16. _____	26. _____
7. _____	17. _____	27. _____
8. _____	18. _____	28. _____
9. _____	19. _____	29. _____
10. _____	20. _____	

42
The Lord's Prayer

"Our (1) who (2) in (3),
(4) be Thy (5).
"Thy (6) come.
Thy (7) be done,
On (8) as it is in (9).
"Give us this (10) our (11) (12).
"And (13) us our debts, as we also have (14) our debtors.
"And do not (15) us into (16), but (17) us from (18). For (19) is
the (20), and the (21), and the (22), forever. Amen.]"

 1. _____   12. _____
 2. _____   13. _____
 3. _____   14. _____
 4. _____   15. _____
 5. _____   16. _____
 6. _____   17. _____
 7. _____   18. _____
 8. _____   19. _____
 9. _____   20. _____
10. _____   21. _____
11. _____   22. _____

43
The Great Commission

"Go (1) and make (2) of all the (3), (4) them in the (5) of the (6) and the (7) and the (8) (9), teaching them to (10) all that I (11) you; and lo, I am with you (12), even to the end of the (13)."

1. _____
2. _____
3. _____
4. _____
5. _____
6. _____
7. _____
8. _____
9. _____
10. _____
11. _____
12. _____
13. _____

44
The Seven Last Sayings from the Cross

(Hint: answers are found in the Gospels)

"My God, My (1), why hast (2) (3) Me?"
"(4), forgive (5); for (6) do not know what they are (7)."
"(8) I say to you, (9) you shall be with (10) in (11)."
"(12), into thy (13) I (14) my (15)."
"Woman, (16), your (17)!" "(18), your (19)!"
"I am (20)."
"It is (21)!"

1. _____   11. _____
2. _____   12. _____
3. _____   13. _____
4. _____   14. _____
5. _____   15. _____
6. _____   16. _____
7. _____   17. _____
8. _____   18. _____
9. _____   19. _____
10. _____   20. _____
                     21. _____

Bible Maze

Follow the Bible verse from the beginning star to the ending star.

Use one continuous line to connect the verse.

You may move from letter to letter in a vertical or horizontal direction. Do not move in a diagonal direction.

45
Fear

Follow the Bible verse to find out why we should not fear.

T	F	D	*	M	F	N	E	F	I	G	H	T
O	N	O	H	E	O	O	G	I	I	S	N	I
T	A	R	T	M	R	E	O	I	D	O	G	N
F	E	A	H	F	T	H	T	S	D	G	F	G
E	R	R	T	O	R	R	U	O	Y	R	O	F
A	O	E	H	E	T	H	E	R	D	U	N	O
R	L	E	M	M	F	E	L	O	R	O	E	R
T	T	H	M	R	O	R	E	L	E	Y	F	Y
H	R	O	F	T	H	T	H	L	R	D	I	O
E	M	F	O	R	T	T	E	L	O	D	*	U

Guilty

Follow the Bible verse to find out how God will deal with the guilty.

```
A  *  A  N  D  T  H  E  L  E  A  N  S  L  E
N  A  N  L  L  B  E  N  O  M  A  E  L  T  E
D  T  D  I  M  L  B  Y  R  E  A  N  E  A  V
T  H  E  W  I  L  N  O  D  W  I  L  L  B  E
H  L  R  D  N  L  A  T  L  I  U  G  E  H  T
E  L  O  L  Y  B  E  Y  N  U  N  U  I  L  T
L  O  R  I  N  O  M  U  N  P  U  I  N  U  Y
O  R  D  W  L  B  Y  N  P  A  N  I  S  H  E
R  D  W  I  L  Y  N  O  M  E  A  N  S  *  D
```

Seek God

Follow the Bible verse to find out when to seek God.

```
E E * S E E A C D N U O F E B Y A M
K E L E E K L L U P O N H I L E H E
T H O E K T H E L O R D W M E I S N
E H T K T H D D C A L W I W L E O E
L D W H L E R N A I N H I H I H P A
O R D W O L O U L H O M M W E E U R
R E B H R E F O L W P L E H I L L *
D W Y I D B F U U N U D H I C A L L
I H A L W Y B N P O L N E L D N U O
L E M E E A Y D C A L U M A Y B E F
E H E H E M A Y B E F O U N D C A L
```

Knowledge

Follow the Bible verses to find out where knowledge begins.

```
*   T   H   E   G   I   N   N   I   N   G   O   F
T   H   E   F   E   A   R   O   F   T   H   E   K
H   E   F   E   B   E   H   T   S   I   D   O   N
E   A   R   L   R   O   F   T   H   E   R   G   O
F   E   A   R   O   F   T   H   E   L   O   N   W
E   O   R   D   I   B   E   G   I   N   N   I   L
A   L   D   R   D   E   G   N   N   I   N   G   E
R   E   I   O   I   H   I   N   N   K   F   O   D
O   H   S   L   S   T   G   N   I   O   W   L   G
F   T   H   E   K   F   O   F   K   N   L   *   E
```

Clean

Follow the Bible verse to find out how God can cleanse you.

```
C   *   C   R   E   A   T   E   I   E   A
R   E   R   T   O   T   E   M   N   H   R
E   A   A   I   G   E   C   L   N       T
A   T   E   I   O   I   C   L   E   A   O
T   E   H   N   D   N   M   W   I   T   G
E   I   N   M   A   M   I   T   H   H   O
I   N   A   E   N   E   R   I   I   I   D
N   M   E   C   D   A   I   I   N   N   M
M   A   L   C   R   C   P   I   R   N   E
E   A   C   L   E   L   S   T   S   P   *
A   N   H   E   N   E   N   A       P   T
C   A   E   W   R   A   H   F       S   S
L   E   A   A   S   T   E   A   D   F   A
```

50
Belief

Follow the Bible verse to find out what happens when you believe in Jesus.

```
B   *   B   E   L   I   E   V   I
E   S   E   L   I   E   V   E   N
L   E   L   I   Y   O   U   I   N
I   J   I   E   D   N   A   H   T
E   D   E   O   Y   Y   S   A   H
V   R   V   U   E   S   U   N   E
E   O   E   S   J   E   S   D   L
I   L   I   H   D   B   E   Y   O
N   E   N   A   L   L   J   O   R
T   H   E   L   O   R   D   U   D
H   D   R   L   R   D   J   E   D
E   L   O   B   E   S   A   V   *
```

51
Grace

Follow the Bible verse to find out about God's grace.

```
*  F  O  R  B  G  R  E  E  B  E  E  N  S  A  V  E
O  O  Y  B  Y  G  R  A  C  E  Y  O  U  H  A  V  E
B  R  E  C  E  R  A  C  E  E  V  A  T  D  N  E  B
Y  G  R  A  Y  A  C  E  Y  O  U  H  H  A  A  B  E
G  D  T  O  T  O  N  T  A  H  T  D  N  A  H  E  E
R  E  H  F  F  D  N  A  E  C  A  R  G  H  T  E  N
A  V  V  Y  B  E  E  E  D  T  H  R  O  U  I  N  S
C  A  A  O  G  O  N  V  F  H  E  G  G  A  N  A
E  S  H  U  O  F  S  A  O  T  H  E  I  H  F  A  V
Y  O  U  R  D  G  I  F  T  S  G  G  F  G  A  H  E
O  N  E  S  E  L  V  E  O  I  O  I  T  U  I  T  D
U  E  E  N  F  O  T  S  I  T  D  F  T  O  F  G  O
H  V  B  O  G  I  F  I  T  I  S  T  T  R  G  U  D
A  V  E  B  E  E  N  S  A  V  E  D  T  H  R  O  *
```

52
All Have Sinned

Follow the Bible verse to find out if everyone is a sinner.

F	*	F	O	R	D	A	N	D	F
O	N	I	N	A	E	N	D	A	A
R	E	S	L	L	N	D	D	A	L
A	V	A	H	L	N	F	E	N	L
L	A	V	V	H	I	N	N	D	S
L	H	A	V	E	S	N	R	O	H
H	A	E	N	N	I	E	T	E	O
N	V	G	E	H	T	F	O	H	R
N	E	L	Y	O	F	G	F	T	*
I	S	O	R	Y	O	F	G	O	D

Faith

Follow the Bible verse to find out what faith means.

```
O  N  *  N  O  W  N  G  S  N  O  F  T  H  I
W  F  W  O  W  F  I  I  I  O  O  N  V  O  N
F  F  F  W  F  A  H  I  T  O  C  E  H  N  G
A  I  T  F  A  I  T  F  C  O  O  N  T  O  S
I  H  I  S  T  H  O  I  V  N  O  R  I     N
T  H  A  S  T  E  P  E  D  O  O  T  O
I  I  R  T  H  E  A  C  O  P  E  D  F  C  T
S  S  V  N  E  F  S  N  H  T  O  D  O  I  S
T  T  S  S  A  O  S  A  S  G  N  T  R  V  E
H  H  U  H  T  E  U  R  T  T  I  H  O  E  E
E  E  R  A  N  C  E  O  F  T  H  E  C  *  N
```

54
Humility

Follow the Bible verse to find out how God rewards humility.

H	*	H	U	L	E	Y	O	U	R	S	E
U	B	U	M	B	Y	S	E	V	L	E	L
M	B	L	E	Y	O	U	R	S	E	L	V
B	L	O	R	D	U	R	L	V	L	V	E
L	E	H	E	L	O	S	E	E	V	E	S
E	H	T	L	E	R	A	D	H	E	W	I
Y	T	F	N	P	D	A	N	I	S	L	L
O	F	O	I	N	T	H	E	T	I	N	L
U	V	E	N	I	N	E	H	T	N	T	E
R	L	C	E	O	R	P	R	E	S	A	X
S	E	N	E	S	E	S	O	Y	T	L	O
E	L	V	E	S	I	*	U	U	Y	T	Y

Chronological Order

Number the events in the order in which they occurred.

55
Time Travel

_____ The children of Israel enter Canaan after forty years in
the wilderness.

_____ The Red Sea parts.

_____ Esau sells his birthright.

_____ Moses dies.

_____ Lot's wife turns into a pillar of salt.

_____ The great flood

_____ The Ten Commandments are given to Moses.

_____ God stops Abraham from sacrificing Isaac.

_____ The great plagues in Egypt

_____ Joseph is sold into slavery.

56
Genesis

Place the following events in the order they appear in Scripture.

_____ God takes Enoch.

_____ Cain settles in Nod.

_____ God creates birds.

_____ Seth is born.

_____ Adam dies.

_____ God tells Noah to build the ark.

_____ Cain kills Abel.

_____ God creates fruit trees.

_____ God is sorry that He made human beings.

_____ Enoch is born.

57
Order of Old Testament

Place the following books in the order in which they appear in the Old Testament.

_____ Hosea

_____ Jeremiah

_____ Lamentations

_____ Ecclesiastes

_____ Isaiah

_____ Amos

_____ Daniel

_____ Song of Solomon

_____ Ezekiel

_____ Joel

58
Who Was Born First?

_____ Aaron
_____ Isaac
_____ Noah
_____ Moses
_____ Esau
_____ Reuben
_____ Jacob
_____ Shem
_____ Benjamin
_____ Joseph

59
Daniel's Life

Place the events of Daniel's life in chronological order.

_____ Daniel's friends are put in the furnace.

_____ Darius appoints Daniel commissioner.

_____ Nebuchadnezzar is removed as king.

_____ Daniel is put in the lion's den.

_____ Daniel chooses vegetables over the king's food.

_____ Nebuchadnezzar appoints Daniel ruler over the province of Babylon.

_____ Daniel interprets the statue dream.

_____ Daniel interprets the handwriting on the wall.

_____ Daniel interprets the tree dream.

60
Jesus' Last Week

Place the events of Jesus' last week in chronological order.

_____ Jesus appears before Pilate.

_____ Passover Dinner

_____ Peter denies Christ.

_____ Jesus approves tribute to Caesar.

_____ Jesus is arrested.

_____ Jesus appears before Herod.

_____ Jesus gives His last sermon.

_____ Jesus curses the fig tree.

_____ Mary anoints Jesus.

_____ Institution of the Lord's Supper

61
Paul's Life

Place the events of Paul's life in chronological order.

_____ Baptized by Ananias

_____ Converts a jailer at Philippi

_____ Starts missionary journey with Barnabas

_____ Blinded by a vision

_____ Converts Lydia

_____ Approves of Stephen's stoning

_____ Preaches on Mars Hill

_____ Meets Timothy who accompanies Paul

_____ Starts missionary journey with Silas

62
Jesus

Place the events of Jesus' life in the order they appear in the Gospels.

_____ Jesus is baptized in the Jordan River.

_____ John the Baptist is born.

_____ Jesus is tempted to worship the devil.

_____ Mary and Joseph travel to Bethlehem.

_____ Zacharias is made silent because of his unbelief.

_____ Jesus is tempted to turn a stone into bread.

_____ Gabriel tells Mary that she will conceive God's Son.

_____ Jesus is born.

_____ Jesus preaches the Sermon on the Mount.

_____ The Holy Spirit descends upon Jesus like a dove.

63
Order of New Testament

Place the following books in the order in which they appear in the New Testament.

_____ Galatians

_____ Titus

_____ 2 Timothy

_____ James

_____ 1 Thessalonians

_____ Ephesians

_____ Philemon

_____ Colossians

_____ Hebrews

_____ Philippians

64
Miscellaneous Events

Place the following in chronological order.

_____ Paul is converted on the road to Damascus.

_____ The mount of transfiguration

_____ The crucifixion

_____ The Day of Pentecost

_____ Satan tempts Jesus.

_____ Peter cuts the ear off a soldier.

_____ A new twelfth disciple is elected.

_____ The Sermon on the Mount

_____ Peter walks on the water.

_____ Peter denies Christ.

Message Puzzles

To find the message in these puzzles, cross out the code letters given at the beginning of each one. Read the remaining letters from left to right. Then write the verse in the white space remaining on the page.

65
God Is Mighty

Cross out the letters K, M, P, U, and V to find the message.

K	U	D	O	M	V	N	O	V	K	K
T	K	F	V	K	K	E	V	P	U	V
P	A	R	P	O	P	L	A	M	N	V
D	M	R	E	U	J	V	O	P	M	I
M	C	E	M	A	N	U	D	B	E	P
G	U	L	K	V	A	K	P	K	U	D
F	O	R	M	P	K	T	U	V	K	H
E	P	M	L	O	M	K	R	D	P	H
A	S	U	K	P	D	M	P	U	M	O
K	N	E	U	M	G	R	E	V	P	A
T	U	T	H	I	M	P	N	G	S	M

66
Wisdom

Cross out the letters P, C, V, and J to find the message.

V	H	O	W	V	C	P	B
L	J	E	P	C	J	P	S
S	P	C	E	C	D	J	V
I	S	P	V	J	V	T	C
J	H	V	C	E	P	C	P
M	C	P	A	P	C	J	V
P	N	J	V	W	H	O	C
F	C	P	I	C	P	V	J
V	N	J	V	P	D	C	V
S	P	V	W	C	I	P	C
J	S	D	P	J	C	O	V
P	C	M	C	A	N	D	P
T	V	P	H	P	V	P	J
V	E	C	J	M	A	C	V
J	P	N	P	C	V	W	H
O	P	C	V	G	A	J	P
V	I	J	P	C	J	N	S
U	N	V	C	C	D	E	P
C	P	R	S	T	A	V	J
J	N	P	D	J	I	N	G

67
God Delivers

Cross out the letters C, B, Q, X, and J to find the message.

```
        I   C   S   O   U   X   G
      H   Q   T   X   T   H   E   J   L
    O   R   J   B   D   X   A   C   N   C   D
  H   E   B   A   N   S   W   J   E   R   C   B   J
E   D   X   M   E   J   X   B   A   C   X   Q   N   Q   X
D   C   X   D   B   Q   E   L   Q   I   X   V   E   J   C
  R   E   Q   D   X   M   E   B   J   F   R   J   B
    J   O   C   M   J   C   A   L   B   L   C
      B   Q   M   C   Y   X   F   J   X
        E   Q   A   R   S   C   Q
```

68
Stand Firm

Cross out the letters B, F, K, P, and U to find the message.

```
                    H
              E  F  W
           H  O  U  I  S
        N  K  O  T  B  W  I
     T  H  M  E  F  I  K  P  S
  A  K  K  G  A  U  I  N  F  S  K
B F  T  B  P  M  E  F  K  B  U  F  B
```

Repent

Cross out the letters B, K, Q, X, and Z to find the message.

```
                        G
                  O  B  D
               I  Q  S  Z  N
            Q  Z  O  B  X  K  Z
         K  W  K  Z  D  Q  E  C  X
      B  L  B  A  R  K  I  B  K  N  B
   G  X  T  Z  K  Q  O  X  M  E  N  Z  X
         X  T  B  H  A  Z  T
         B  A  K  Q  B  K  L
         L  X  E  X  V  Q  E
         Q  R  Y  W  K  Z  B
         H  Z  K  B  E  Q  R
         E  Q  X  S  K  X  K
         K  H  B  X  Z  B  O
         Z  Q  U  K  L  Q  D
         B  R  Z  Q  E  X  Z
         P  Q  E  X  B  N  T
```

Love

Cross out the letters W, Q, F, Y, and C to find the message.

```
              L     W     O
              F     V     E
              I     S     P
              Y     A     T
              I     C     E
              Q     N     F
 T  Y  L  O   C     V     E   C  I  S  Y
 K  I  W  N   Q     D     Y   A  N  D  W
 Q  Y  I  S   F     C     N   W  O  T  C
 J  E  C  A   L     O     C   U  Y  W  F
              S     F     L
              O     V     E
              D     Q     O
              C     E     S
              N     W     O
              Y     T     F
              B     C     R
              A     G     A
              F     N     D
              W     N     Q
              S     I     O
              T     Y     A
              R     Q     R
              O     G     A
              W     N     T
```

71
Burdens

Cross out the letters G, J, K, M, V, and Y to find the message.

```
B   M   E   Y   G   Y   A   R   G   K   O   N   V
V   E   K   G   A   N   V   Y   O   J   G   Y   M
T   H   G   J   E   G   R   K   J   V   S   K   B
G   M   U   R   V   M   D   E   M   N   Y   G   Y
S   V   M   A   N   D   G   Y   K   G   T   H   K
Y   U   S   Y   F   U   L   F   K   M   V   J   M
M   G   I   L   L   M   T   Y   G   H   Y   J   V
E   V   M   L   A   K   K   W   J   Y   M   J   O
K   F   G   Y   V   C   H   Y   K   R   J   G   I
G   K   S   T   K   J   M   J   Y   G   M   J   V
```

Resist the Devil

Cross out the letters C, K, P, Q, and X to find the message.

```
S  C  K  U  C  P
C  B  P  Q  K  X
M  C  I  X  Q  K
C  C  T  K  P  C
T  K  X  P  X  Q
P  Q  H  Q  C  K
X  E  C  C  R  P
E  C  F  P  Q  Q
X  O  C  K  P  X
Q  X  R  E  C  P
T  K  P  Q  X  Q
C  O  K  K  G  X
P  Q  O  D  X  C
R  K  P  Q  E  C  Q  S  I  X  X  S  T  Q  P  X  Q
X  T  P  H  Q  X  E  X  Q  D  P  X  C  E  K  X  P
V  C  P  Q  I  C  L  K  Q  X  A  P  K  K  N  Q  P
K  D  P  H  E  X  K  W  X  P  Q  I  C  L  C  K  L
P  K  F  L  Q  C  E  E  Q  X  F  R  X  K  O  Q  X
C  K  P  Q  M  X  Q  P  Y  C  K  P  O  U  C  K  P
```

Word Search

Use the word list found before each puzzle to help you find all the words.
Strike through each word found. The word list is your answer sheet.

73
Old Testament Prophets

Hosea	Ezekiel
Obadiah	Amos
Jonah	Nahum
Joel	Elijah
Micah	Daniel

```
A  O  P  N  B  J  R  E  S  K  Q
S  J  R  E  O  Z  F  C  G  V  H
U  T  Y  E  W  L  Y  K  W  V  G
M  O  L  Q  Z  J  L  H  B  F  C
L  I  V  T  F  E  L  I  J  A  H
X  H  P  D  I  A  K  T  I  U  X
B  A  H  N  L  Z  M  I  C  A  H
R  I  A  U  A  M  O  S  E  U  O
M  D  K  I  Q  H  D  H  A  L  S
H  A  N  O  J  M  U  G  K  R  E
C  B  Z  O  T  P  S  M  D  N  A
H  O  E  B  L  N  T  O  V  L  W
```

Kings

Hezekiah

Ahab

Nadab

Asa

Hoshea

Uzziah

Jeroboam

Manasseh

Joash

Elah

```
G   U   M   A   N   A   S   S   E   H   J
P   N   Z   G   B   I   M   F   B   K   O
B   H   E   Z   E   K   I   A   H   K   A
V   A   O   U   I   T   H   S   Y   L   S
J   X   D   D   N   A   E   H   S   O   H
C   F   D   A   C   S   H   L   E   Z   A
H   B   Q   E   N   A   I   J   R   H   L
A   M   A   O   B   O   R   E   J   A   E
```

75
Jacob's Sons

Joseph	Zebulun
Gad	Benjamin
Reuben	Simeon
Levi	Judah
Asher	Dan

```
I   R   J   Q   B   O   S   D   L
H   Z   E   B   U   L   U   N   I
P   B   H   U   E   C   O   A   V
E   G   E   V   B   E   T   D   K
S   R   I   N   M   E   A   Z   G
O   P   E   I   J   G   N   R   A
J   B   S   H   N   A   C   A   M
Y   E   O   F   S   U   M   J   E
N   I   J   U   D   A   H   I   O
L   F   X   K   D   M   W   H   N
```

Mountains

Carmel
Tabor
Hermon
Sinai

Pisgah
Zion
Nebo
Ararat

C	I	Z	K	I	H	X	V	J	G
F	J	L	I	L	N	A	D	W	I
N	N	E	B	O	R	N	M	A	P
M	J	M	M	A	N	P	N	U	B
T	O	R	R	H	I	I	D	C	I
Q	E	A	G	W	S	S	L	A	S
H	T	C	E	S	Y	G	B	V	E
S	Z	V	O	X	T	A	B	O	R
Y	P	R	Q	Z	A	H	R	T	F

77
Trees

Poplar
Cypress
Fig
Sycamore
Aloe
Cedar

Juniper
Almond
Fir
Pomegranate
Oak
Olive

```
E  R  E  P  I  N  U  J  E  E  A  O
O  T  K  F  Y  X  I  R  V  G  L  Q
P  J  A  A  L  M  O  N  D  I  P  D
A  Q  R  N  L  M  W  J  V  O  P  H
L  E  T  U  A  G  H  E  Z  W  M  S
O  S  F  C  S  R  A  L  P  O  P  M
E  R  Y  C  S  D  G  V  I  B  P  C
N  S  E  Q  E  U  N  E  T  Z  J  R
T  M  F  I  R  D  Y  K  M  U  X  L
F  C  I  E  P  B  A  G  C  O  X  K
N  L  G  O  Y  A  H  R  W  R  A  Y
D  O  A  P  C  K  B  I  S  Z  A  V
```

Disciples

Peter   Matthew
Simon   Philip
John   Andrew
James   Thomas
Judas   Bartholomew

```
A  S  I  M  Z  N  A  T  H  L  B  I
S  O  P  P  H  I  L  I  P  A  S  W
A  D  F  O  Z  R  V  Y  R  C  E  H
D  D  J  L  I  B  F  T  H  H  R  F
U  V  S  K  J  L  H  F  T  R  J  O
J  O  S  I  M  O  N  T  Q  E  D  K
O  J  M  Q  L  A  A  O  Z  T  N  G
S  A  S  O  M  M  X  W  J  E  G  P
L  M  M  A  N  D  R  E  W  P  B  F
P  E  S  A  M  O  H  T  Z  O  O  F
W  S  D  A  K  O  N  G  W  K  L  P
```

Countries and Towns

Cana	Samaria
Judea	Galilee
Ephesus	Rome
Nazareth	Bethany
Jerusalem	Philippi
Capernaum	Jericho

```
J  X  J  M  U  O  G  U  C  S  B  K  A  N
E  E  N  U  T  V  J  A  U  R  P  Z  P  A
R  A  M  Z  D  I  P  S  L  Q  H  A  E  Z
U  N  F  O  L  E  E  O  X  I  I  J  I  A
S  A  M  V  R  H  A  C  Q  R  L  H  S  R
A  C  D  N  P  H  C  K  A  P  I  E  E  E
L  N  A  E  B  A  Y  M  T  D  P  W  E  T
E  U  B  E  T  H  A  N  Y  S  P  L  F  H
M  A  W  E  G  S  R  J  E  R  I  C  H  O
```

80
New Testament Women

Mary
Priscilla
Eunice
Martha
Phoebe

Herodias
Claudia
Bernice
Lydia
Sapphira

```
G  C  A  L  L  I  C  S  I  R  P  A  B
D  P  A  O  Y  R  A  M  K  V  I  E  A
I  H  B  I  C  I  C  X  N  D  R  Y  M
E  O  H  O  D  Q  J  P  U  N  Z  S  A
R  E  P  O  N  Y  F  A  I  U  L  K  R
U  B  R  T  M  P  L  C  W  B  E  D  T
G  E  U  N  I  C  E  F  O  Q  J  L  H
H  T  A  F  R  S  A  P  P  H  I  R  A
```

81
Miracles

Wine
Bread
Fig
Leper
Water

Blind
Risen
Fish
Lazarus
Storm

```
W   Y   O   H   O   A   R   N   F
B   I   I   J   L   I   M   Z   S
G   L   N   T   S   A   P   U   T
R   D   L   E   P   A   R   I   O
U   A   N   Q   W   E   T   E   R
C   E   K   M   Z   A   H   D   M
T   R   U   A   C   N   S   B   X
R   B   L   I   N   O   I   H   E
D   G   R   F   G   I   F   K   D
```

Peter's Life

Rock   Disciple
Dorcas   Preacher
Cephas   Fisherman
Denial   Pentecost
Prison   Andrew

```
E  J  Q  D  I  O  T  L  X  T  F
N  A  M  R  E  H  S  I  F  S  F  R
O  W  S  P  R  U  B  C  G  O  R  K
S  K  G  C  G  W  N  G  D  C  K  Z
I  P  H  S  E  V  C  E  O  E  Q
R  G  R  R  Y  P  N  R  R  T  Q  B
P  S  D  E  M  I  H  S  C  N  J
U  N  H  R  A  W  Q  A  A  E  W
A  P  Z  L  L  C  E  X  S  P  T
J  F  A  K  T  N  H  A  O  F  M  C
D  I  S  C  I  P  L  E  T  U  C
B  L  V  D  C  S  M  Z  R  Y  S
```

Answers

1

Amos
Psalms
Obadiah
Song of Solomon
Titus
Lamentations
Ezra

2

Water
Oldest
Red Sea
Serpent
Hail
Insects
Pharaoh

3

Rome
Eden
Patmos
Egypt
Nineveh
Tyre

4

Deceit
Envy
Vanity
Idolatry
Lie

5

Bread
Eggs
Almonds
Nuts
Salt

6

God
Eden
Nod
Evil
Serpent
Image
Sin

7

Galatians
Revelation
Acts
Colossians
Ephesians

8

First
Advocate
Immanuel
Teacher
Hope

9

Supper
Unleavened
Passover
Pitcher
Eat
Reclining

10

Crown
Resurrection
Opened
Stone
Skull

11

1. Solomon
2. Jesse
3. Temple
4. Goliath
5. King
6. Bathsheba
Bonus:
    Jonathan

12

1. Joel
2. Enoch
3. Elijah
4. Nathan
5. Micah
6. Nahum
Bonus:
    Jonah

13

1. Tigris
2. Nile
3. Jordan
4. Euphrates
5. Arnon
6. Pishon
Bonus:
   Red Sea

14

1. Uriah
2. Joab
3. Joshua
4. David
5. Abner
6. General
Bonus:
   Gibeon

15

1. Esther
2. Abigail
3. Delilah
4. Rachel
5. Hagar
6. Gomer
Bonus
   Gabriel

16

1. Leaven
2. Widow
3. Sower
4. House
5. Samaritan
6. Talents
Bonus:
   Tares

17

1. Simon
2. Water
3. Pentecost
4. Dorcas
5. Apostle
6. Cock
Bonus:
   Andrew

18

1. Patience
2. Wisdom
3. Prayer
4. lFaith
5. Mercy
6. LRepentance
7. Confession
8. Trials
9. Righteousness
10. Baptism
Bonus:
   Obedience

19

1. Pilate
2. Blood
3. Cross
4. Golgotha
5. Garments
6. Crown
Bonus:
   Simon

20

1. Saul
2. Ananias
3. Colossians
4. Tentmaker
5. Silas
6. Blinded
Bonus:
   Damascus

21

1. g
2. e
3. a
4. j
5. c
6. h
7. d
8. i
9. b
10. f

22	23	24	25
1. f	1. f	1. c	1. d
2. e	2. a	2. a	2. b
3. i	3. d	3. d	3. e
4. h	4. c	4. e	4. f
5. c	5. b	5. f	5. a
6. j	6. e	6. b	6. c
7. b			
8. a			
9. g			
10. d			

26	27	28	29
1. h	1. e	Matthew 7:7	Proverbs 15:1
2. d	2. h		
3. g	3. a		
4. f	4. f		
5. b	5. g		
6. c	6. b		
7. a	7. d		
8. e	8. c		

30	31	32	33
Philippians 4:13	2 Peter 1:21	Psalms 84:11	1 John 5:13

34	35	36	37
Jeremiah 29:11	2 Timothy 3:16	Isaiah 53:6	1 John 1:9

38
Proverbs 3:5-6
1. Trust
2. Lord
3. heart
4. lean
5. own
6. understanding
7. ways
8. acknowledge
9. paths
10. straight

39
Psalsm 100:1-3
1. Shout
2. joyfully
3. earth
4. Serve
5. gladness
6. Come
7. joyful
8. singing
9. Know
10. Himself
11. made
12. ourselves
13. His
14. people
15. sheep

40
Exodus 20:3-17

1. gods
2. Me
3. idol
4. likeness
5. heaven
6. water
7. worship
8. serve
9. jealous
10. iniquity
11. generations
12. hate
13. lovingkindness
14. love
15. keep
16. name
17. vain
18. unpunished
19. name
20. vain
21. sabbath
22. holy
23. Six
24. seventh
25. sabbath
26. cattle
27. six
28. heavens
29. earth
30. sea
31. seventh
32. sabbath
33. holy
34. Honor
35. prolonged
36. murder
37. commit
38. adultery
39. steal
40. false
41. witness
42. witness
43. wife
44. belongs

41
Matthew 5:3-12

1. poor
2. kingdom
3. mourn
4. comforted
5. gentle
6. inherit
7. hunger
8. thirst
9. righteousness
10. satisfied
11. merciful
12. mercy
13. pure
14. see
15. peacemakers
16. sons
17. persecuted
18. righteousness
19. kingdom
20. heaven
21. men
22. revile
23. persecute
24. evil
25. falsely
26. Rejoice
27. reward
28. persecuted
29. prophets

42
Matthew 6:9-13

1. Father
2. art
3. heaven
4. Hallowed
5. name
6. kingdom
7. will
8. earth
9. heaven
10. day
11. daily
12. bread
13. forgive
14. forgiven
15. lead
16. temptation
17. deliver
18. evil
19. Thine
20. kingdom
21. power
22. glory

43
Matthew 28:19-20

1. therefore
2. disciples
3. nations
4. baptizing
5. name
6. Father
7. Son
8. Holy
9. Spirit
10. commanded
11. commanded
12. always
13. age

44

Matthew 27:46; Luke 23:34,43,46; John 19:26-27,28,30
1. God
2. Thou
3. forsaken
4. Father
5. them
6. they
7. doing
8. Truly
9. today
10. Me
11. Paradise
12. Father
13. hands
14. commit
15. Spirit
16. behold
17. son
18. Behold
19. mother
20. thirsty
21. finished

45

Deuteronomy 3:22

```
      D *        N E F I G H T
O N O            O             I
T                E   I D O     N
F E A            H T S G G
    R T                R     F
    H E                U     O
      M F              O     R
        O R            Y     Y
        T H     R D          O
        E L O       *   U
```

46

Nahum 1:3

```
A *              E A N S
N              N O M       L
D          L B Y           E A V
T      W I L                   E
H    R D       T L I U G E H T
E L O          Y
               U N P U
                 N I S H E
                     * D
```

47

Isaiah 55:6

```
    * S
      E
      E                              I S N
E H T K                        E         E
L                    N H I     H         A
O R D W                O   M W E R
      H   E F O         P       H I L   *
      I   B   U         U
      L   Y   N         L
      E   A   D C A L
      H E M
```

48

Proverbs 1:7

```
*          G I N N I N G O F
T          E                 K
H E        B E H T S I D     N
H                    R       O
F E A R O F T H E L O        W
                             L
                             E
                             D
                             G
                         *   E
```

49

Psalm 51:10

```
C   *
R       R T O
E       A   G
A       E   O
T       H   D         W   I T
E       N   A       I T       H
I       A   N       R         I
N       E   D       I         N   M
M       L   R       P         M E
E A C   R   E       S T S     *
            E N           S A
            W N           A F
            A S T E A D       F
```

50

Acts 16:31

```
B
E
L
I              D N     A
E          O Y         S
V          U           U
E          S           S
I          H           E
N          A           J
T  H E  L  O R D
           L         E  D
           B E S A V  *
```

51

Ephesians 2:8-9

```
*  F
   O
B  R
Y
G      O T O N T A H T D N A H
R      F                     T
A      Y                     I
C      O                     A
E      U           T H E   H F
Y      R           S   G   G
O      S E L V E   I   I   U
U          S I T   F  T O F G O D
H                     R       D
A V E B E E N S A V E D T H   *
```

52

Romans 3:23

```
F  *         D A N D F
O            E       A
R            N       L
A            N       L
L            I       S
L  H A V E   S    R O H
                  T
   G E H T F O
   L              *
   O R Y O F G O D
```

53

Hebrews 11:1

```
O  N  *                    N  O  F  T  H     I
W                       I  O              H  N  G
F           T           T     C  E  H        G
A  I  T                 C        O     T     S
   H  I                 I  V  N     T  R     N
      S                             O     O
      T  H              O  P  E  D  F        T
         E              H                    S
   S  S  A              S  G        N        E
   U                          I             E
   R  A  N  C  E  O  F  T  H        *        N
```

54

James 4:10

```
H  *
U
M  B  L  E  Y  O  U  R  S        E
                                L
      H  E  L     O              V
         F           R     D  H  E  W     I
      T  O           D  A  N        S        L
      O                             I        L
      E              E     H  T  N           E
      C              R  P                 A  X
      N  E  S  E        O  Y  T  L
                     *  U
```

55	56	57	58	59
10	8	8	9	4
7	4	4	3	8
4	2	5	1	6
9	6	1	10	9
2	7	3	4	1
1	10	10	6	3
8	3	7	5	2
3	1	2	2	7
6	9	6	8	5
5	5	9	7	

60	61	62	63	64
9	3	6	1	10
5	8	3	7	4
8	4	9	6	7
2	2	4	10	9
7	7	1	5	1
10	1	8	2	5
3	9	2	8	8
1	6	5	4	2
4	5	10	9	3
6		7	3	6

65
Joel 2:21

66
Proverbs 3:13

67
Psalm 34:4

68
Matthew 12:30

69
Acts 17:30

70
1 Corinthians 13:4

71
Galatians 6:2

72
James 4:7